3 Day Green Smoothie Detox

The Faster, Better, Stronger Weight Loss Plan

Liz Swann Miller
www.Greensmoothies.me

Table of Contents

Believe in yourself! Have faith in your abilities! Without a humble but reasonable confidence in your own powers you cannot be successful or happy.

– Norman Vincent Peale

Get Ready To Detox!

Welcome! I am so glad you decided to join me on your journey into a stronger, healthier more vibrant you!

In this book I'll cover everything you need to take a safe and successful 3 Day Green Smoothie Cleanse. You are going to learn all about detoxifying your body, and how you can feel better and look better than you have in years – and in only 72 hours.

Detoxifying using greens such as parsley has been done in some cultures for thousands of years. Smoothie-like fruit beverages have been popular since the first mechanical blending machines were invented in the early decades of the 20th century. So, why not combine the two and get a two-for-one double whammy?

Don't worry; there are no starvation diets here. You will feel full and have lots of energy, and after 3 days you will feel great. You might even find that you've lost a pound or two; which is one my favorite by-products of going on a detox.

A Green Smoothie detox is very simply, just having your Green Smoothies for every meal and your snacks instead of regular food. It means drinking lots of water (with lemon, and you can drink coconut water too), and drinking herbal teas. Ginger, Peppermint or whatever kind you like as long as it is caffeine free and without any added sweeteners. (Tip – Black and Green teas have caffeine in them so make sure you don't drink them while detoxing.)

A cleanse removes all of the built-up toxins from your body. When your body is full of those toxins, it can make you feel sluggish and bloated, and it saps all the energy right out of you. If you have digestive system issues such as indigestion, constipation, flatulence or acid reflux symptoms, a Green Smoothie detox can help clear these problems right up.

Green Smoothies are also fabulous at:
- boosting your immune system
- cleaning your blood
- flushing out the kidneys and liver
- improving your concentration
- enhancing your moods
- helping to reduce stress
- and prevent diseases and premature aging.

After a Green Smoothie detox, you will probably find that you sleep better, have fewer allergies, the tone and texture of your skin is much better and you have fewer blemishes.

There is absolutely nothing wrong with a detox, as long as you do it in a healthy way.

Detoxing is usually recommended no more than 4 times per year for a continuous 3 to 4 day period. I personally prefer to detox for 3 days, as I feel I get the full benefits within this time frame. Just add a detox to your seasonal calendar, and do one at the beginning of each season.

That once in a while detox, makes eating healthy the rest of the time, seem so much easier. There is nothing wrong with throwing in an extra 1 day detox from time to time if you feel that you have had a little more than you should have of the "not so good stuff" to eat.

One of the first things that most people ask is, "Why not detox by fasting or juicing?" There are reasons why I don't do either of these. Fasting can be very hard on your body and mind. This literally is a starvation diet detox. A juice detox is more nutritious than a fast, but you miss out on the fiber of whole fruit and the vitamins, antioxidants and other nutrients that you get in the greens and vegetables that actually promote the cleansing action.

Detoxing with Green Smoothies is really not going to be much different than the Green Smoothies you have daily. It is just a matter of adjusting the ingredients to get the maximum cleansing benefit. Detoxing is not harmful as long as you use the right ingredients to provide all of the nutrients and calories that your body needs to function efficiently.

The will to win, the desire to succeed, the urge to reach your full potential… these are the keys that will unlock the door to personal excellence.

– Conficius

How I Started With Green Smoothies!

I have always believed that there is a deep connection between the foods we eat, and the way we feel. In my early twenties I was severely overweight, depressed and cranky most of the time. To be quite honest, I was all of the above most of my childhood, and teen years as well.

When I was in college I was so tired all of the time, I missed most of my classes and eventually flunked out my first year. I was suffering from high cholesterol, obesity, and had the attention span of a bumble bee. Trying to effectively cope with the pressures of exams and life in general I turned to sweet, salty and fried comfort foods to escape from it all.

I knew I wasn't making the best decisions, but the emotional connection to food was just too hard to break at the time. It soon became a vicious circle from which I could not, and did not want to escape from.

I think they call that depression these days, which only leads to more of the same.

At this point in my life I was at a crossroads where I had the choice to either keep on living the way I was (overweight, tired and not happy with my body), or get an entirely new life plan! I was about to get married to my wonderful husband, and I decided that my marriage would symbolize a whole series of new beginnings.

I thought, "What better way to get healthier than become an expert in all-natural therapies?" So, I enrolled in a 4 year curriculum to become a licensed naturopath. Over the course of those 4 years I learned all about the human body, and how to heal it using natural approaches that treat problems from the root and not only the symptoms.

The more I learned, the healthier I became. I cut out dairy products, gluten and processed foods almost completely from my diet, and started eating more fruits, vegetables and whole foods. I couldn't believe how much stronger and better I felt physically. The emotional payoffs were even more amazing than that! I lost all of my "baby fat" and even started going to yoga and meditation classes.

When I started treating others in my private practice, I discovered that many women, and even men, felt exactly the same way as I had felt my whole life. They were trying to live the best way they could, but there were too many nutritional "roadblocks" that were standing in the way of better health. Being able to learn more about how people related to food, has taught me even more about how our food choices affect all aspects of our lives.

The Green Smoothie Connection

I discovered the power of eating greens early on in my studies as a Naturopath, but never tried blending them together with fruits! When I tasted my first smoothie I was amazed how tasty and refreshing it was. So I started drinking them on a regular basis. After 2 weeks of drinking a shake a day I was feeling a lot more energized, relaxed and stronger. I've never stopped since!

I started prescribing green smoothies to my clients, and was completely amazed by the results. They were not only fast and easy to make, they were also proving to be a very powerful healing tool that I could use to help people feel better and improve their own lives.

Green smoothies aren't a miracle magic pill, and they won't heal every disease in the world, but they are extremely powerful as a method to provide your body with a quick and easy boost of high level nutrients. The energy and the health benefits are simply amazing, especially when you can get all of this from a simple green smoothie!

Greens Taste Good?

I was never a fan of greens, and maybe you aren't either. And that's exactly where green smoothies come into play. They provide an amazingly tasty way to consume large amounts of greens, without feeling like you're eating an entire forest. With a few little tweaks, even the least adventurous among us can find creative ways to ramp up the taste, while keeping all the benefits of a green smoothie.

Green smoothies are also a great way to introduce a variety of different greens to the younger, more food fussy generation. My daughters love having their special green "Milkshakes" as we like to call them at home.

I want to end with an ancient Buddhist saying – ***"A journey of 1,000 miles begins with a single step"***.

I hope this book will help you take the first step to a stronger and healthier you. Just remember to take it slow and you'll reap the benefits of drinking green smoothies a lot faster than you think.

I am honored to be able to share my findings and experiences with you in this book. Thanks for reading, and I wish you a wonderful and refreshing journey into the world of green smoothies!

What's Inside The 3 Day Smoothie Detox?

Chapter 1	you'll learn all about leafy greens and their health benefits. We will also discuss why they are the main ingredients used in Green Smoothies.
Chapter 2	will have you making perfect, delicious smoothies in no time at all.
Chapter 3	will teach us how to prepare ourselves for a 3 Day Green Smoothie Cleanse.
Chapter 4	is a discussion of possible side effects that some may have when drinking Green Smoothies.
Chapter 5	is a detailed step by step plan, for the 3 Day Green Smoothie Cleanse.
Chapter 6	is where we get our shopping list together and get all of our smoothie supplies ready for our detox.
Chapter 7	has information on blenders that you need to know when making smoothies.
Chapter 8	is where you find all the delicious Green Smoothie recipes to choose from for your detox plan.
Chapter 9	will sum up the information that we have learned in this book.
Chapter 10	contains frequently asked questions about the 3 Day Green Smoothie Cleanse.
The Recipes	Throughout the book you will find different recipes that correspond to specific categories. For quick reference to any of the recipes, find them on the table of contents. If you're reading the digital version of this book, simply click on the recipe you want to prepare on the table of contents and you'll be sent to the corresponding page!

I've tried hard to create low budget recipes that contain both ingredients that are easy to find, easy to prepare, while maintaining maximum taste.

Enjoy!

The Benefits
Of Leafy Greens

Almost everyone knows that leafy green vegetables are really good for them, but most do not realize just exactly how good they are. **Fact:** Leafy Greens contain most of the nutrients that the human body requires and combined with other vegetables and fruits, they can provide a complete and balanced diet.

Because of their slightly bitter flavor, many people choose not to eat them. The truth is that they have nutrients that many other vegetables do not provide. That means that they are vitally important to a balanced diet. This is where Green Smoothies come in to play, because they give you all the benefits and none of the bitter taste. The taste of the greens just disappears into the flavor of the fruits that you mix them with.

Eating your leafy greens whole is always an option for those who like them. However, greens are full of cellulose fibers that are very difficult for the body to break down in order to get to the nutrients they contain. When you have them in Green Smoothie form, your blender does that work for you, allowing your body to take full advantage of the nutrition they offer.

Greens are unique in that they contain Vitamin K. Very few foods can lay claim to that fame. Vitamin K is what allows the body to produce the proteins that are needed for bone health. Vitamin K deficiencies have been linked to birth defects and cancer. Greens also provide other nutrients such as, Vitamins A, C, E and many of the B vitamins, minerals and phytonutrients.

Greens provide you with high levels of amino acids, which are the building blocks of protein. By obtaining your amino acids naturally, the body can create to proteins that it needs, rather than having to break down the complex proteins that are contained in meat. The body has to work twice as hard to digest meat proteins. Leafy greens also provide enzymes that the body needs for good digestion without bloating and flatulence.

Organic greens are always preferable, but it is important that they be fresh, as well. When they begin to wilt, they are losing their nutrients. It is best to chop them or tear them into small pieces before adding them to the blender. They should always be added to your smoothie last.

Following is a list of some of the greens that I choose most often for Green Smoothies. I have included some nutritional information on each one.

- Baby Spinach is one of the best greens to start with, because the flavor is very mild. It contains iron, fiber, protein, calcium and Vitamins A, B9, C, E and K.
- Kale is also very mild in taste and has water, fiber, protein, Vitamins A, K, B1, B2, B3, B5, B9, B12, C, D, E, calcium, iron, magnesium, potassium, phosphorus and manganese.
- Parsley is a great mild herb that contains fiber, protein, VitaminsB1, B2, B3, B55, B6, B9, C, K, calcium, iron, magnesium, phosphorus, potassium and zinc.
- Bok Choy or Chinese Cabbage, has a succulent flavor and is a very popular choice. It provides such nutrients as fiber, protein calcium, iron, magnesium and Vitamins A and C.
- Collard Greens are a relative of broccoli and cabbage. They provide protein, calcium, fiber and Vitamins A, C and K.

- Dandelion Greens are quickly growing in popularity and are commonly used to make many foods and drinks. Their super nutritional properties include; water, fiber, protein, Vitamins A, B1, B2, B3, B5, B6, B9, C, D, E, K, choline, calcium, iron, magnesium, manganese, phosphorus, potassium and zinc.
- Romaine Lettuce is mild and delicious, and contains water, fiber, protein, Vitamins A, B9 and C, calcium, iron, phosphorus and potassium.
- Cilantro is in reality the herb called coriander and has a citrus-like flavor. It contains fiber, protein and Vitamins A and C.
- Mustard Greens are more strongly flavored, but are very popular with those who eat greens regularly. They contain fiber, selenium, chromium, iron and zinc.

This is only a sampling of the many choices in greens that are available. If I tried to include them all here, the list would be very long indeed. You will have to explore greens and their flavors on your own to decide which ones that you prefer. It is easier for the non-green eater to begin making Green Smoothies with the mildest flavored greens. Once you have discovered the delicious goodness of Green Smoothies, then you can experiment with other, different greens.

Greens contain massive amounts of antioxidants, and they are believed to help prevent cancer and heart disease.

Begin by using a handful or two of greens and increase them gradually in your smoothies. Your goal should be to get up to 3 or 4 cups of chopped greens every day. All green vegetables are good for you, and should be included in your diet. However, greens have much less starch than is found in other green vegetables, and will give your Green Smoothie a far better texture. Do not eat just one variety of greens; it is recommended to rotate them, eating at least 7 different kinds each week.

I don't believe you have to be better than everybody else. I believe you have to be better than you ever thought you could be.

– Ken Venturi

How To Create The Perfect Smoothie

Let's get right to making those smoothies, so we can go right on to enjoying them.

Nothing could be simpler or easier than making smoothies. You will be an expert in no time. Once you start, you probably won't be able to stop, I know I couldn't. You'll never be bored with it because there are so many ingredients to choose from, and so many ways to combine them.

Everyone knows how to use a blender; just throw stuff in and power it on. There are some techniques that will help you to get the consistency of your mixture just perfect. Texture, temperature and taste are what make Green Smoothies a satisfying food experience.

8 STEPS to Your Perfect Green Smoothie

1. **Liquid** – Normally liquid is used in smoothies, and except when the recipe directs you differently, it is added first. Some recipes may call for ice.

2. **Base** – The base is fruit. Fruit gives the smoothie a creamy texture and the sweetness that you need. Water based fruits create a thin and runny mixture. The list below shows the best fruits for the base.

3. **Mixing Flavors** – Add your favorite water base fruit here, to enhance your smoothie's sweetness and disguise the bitter taste of the greens. Use strong flavored fruit or several types of fruit. The bigger the variety of fruits that you use the more nutrients you get. Mix and match your favorites.

4. **Additional Ingredients**–flax seeds, wheat germ, Chia Seeds, Goji Berries and sprouts, which also qualify as a green. These are considered Super foods, and have massive amounts of protein, antioxidants, vitamins and minerals. Nuts, herbs, spices and extracts can be added.

5. **Pulse** in the blender a few times to mix before adding greens.

6. **Add The Greens** – Time for the super nutritious ingredients. Add as many as you like. Because of their nutrients, greens are the most important ingredient. The perfect ratio is 40% greens with 60% fruit. Increase the greens gradually, so that you don't overpower your taste buds. You get an A+ if you make it to 70% greens in your smoothies. It doesn't matter, because you won't taste them.

7. **Blend** the mixture on high about 30 seconds or longer, until you get the texture and creaminess you want.

8. **Pour** into a tall cold glass and enjoy your Green Smoothie.

All you need to make smoothies is the blender, a chopping board and a sharp knife. The smaller the pieces of fruit and greens, the less work the blender has to do, and the sooner you will be having your smoothie. This is very important when you are using a generic blender.

Remove cores from pineapples, apples or pears to get a smoother texture. Who needs lumps in their smoothie? Of course, you should not blend the ingredients any more than is necessary to get a smooth texture. Your ingredients will begin to lose their nutrients when exposed to the air.

Liquids that work best in smoothies for detoxifying

Water – Always use filtered or distilled water that has had the chemicals removed.

Coconut Water – Tap and drain the water from a whole coconut. The meat of the coconut is also delicious to add to your smoothie, and is perfect with other tropical fruits. You can purchase coconut water, but check the packaging for unwanted additives.

Nut Milks – These are great added liquids for detox smoothies. Remember to choose ones that are organic if possible and with no added sugar to them. Also, use them in moderation because they contain fats.

Hint: When doing a Green Smoothie detox, don't use the fruit nectars and juices that you normally use on occasion. You will get the same flavor and sweetness from whole ripe fruits, plus the added fiber and nutrients.

Base Fruits for a creamy texture

Banana – Sweet and creamy banana is the #1 preference for the base.

Mango – Tropical is always nice.

Peach – Sweetness and creamy texture.

Pear – Sweet and mildly flavored.

Apple – A choice of sweet or tart; there's an apple for everyone.

Papaya – Another tropical choice. Mix it half and half with mango.

Too many water fruits will make your smoothie watery. The perfect mix of fruit should be one half as much water fruit as base fruit. Example: 2 bananas and 1 cup of strawberries. Add your water fruit a little at a time. When the consistency is perfect, you have added enough.

Adding your greens

Pick greens to suit your nutritional needs, and forget about taste. You will never know they are in there. Any green you like will work, and the more, the better. It is best to rotate 7 different greens every week to fully take advantage of the nutrients they offer.

My preferred greens for a detox include:
- Kale
- Parsley
- Bok Choy
- Spinach
- Dandelion Greens
- Romaine Lettuce

See how easy it is to get everything you need in one Green Smoothie.

Troubleshooting Smoothies

If the smoothie is too sweet – Add more greens, some celery or a little sea salt.

If it's not as cold as you want – Add bananas and berries that are frozen fresh and whole (bananas should not be peeled before freezing, because they will turn black and nasty), or add some crushed ice.

If it tastes bitter – Additional fruit can be added. Bananas, pineapple, ripe berries and sweet oranges will cover that bitter taste completely.

If it is not sweet enough – Add a little sweetener. Try honey (preferably raw) or agave nectar. Sweeteners such as Stevia or Splenda can be used, if you choose. Chopped dates or extra bananas will sweeten it more. Remember, riper fruit makes a sweeter smoothie.

It is not thick enough – Add ¼ of an Avocado or the same amount of coconut meat. Both add some calories, but they are from "good" fats that your body needs. Avocado also adds an extra creaminess to smoothies. More greens will thicken a smoothie.

How To Store Your Smoothies

Smoothies really are not meant to be "prepared in advance." They are at their very best in taste, texture and nutrition when you have them immediately. Vitamins and other nutrients begin to break down from exposure to air, and they lose their potency rapidly.

Should you need to store the smoothie temporarily, or if your recipe makes more than one smoothie–store it in an airtight glass container in the refrigerator. Do not use plastic or metal containers, as your smoothie may absorb unwanted chemicals from these materials, and metals hasten the oxidation of the nutrients. They will keep fairly well for one night or for the time between breakfast and lunch.

When it is time to enjoy your refrigerated smoothie, shake it well, or give it another turn in the blender. The fruit fiber and liquid tends to separate when it sits.

You should never keep a smoothie any longer than 24 hours; throw it out and make yourself another.

If you can dream it, you can do it.

– Walt Disney

Getting Ready
For A Smoothie Detox

While there are no complicated preparations necessary before you begin your 3 Day Green Smoothie Detox, there are some things to consider that will make it easier.

A 3 Day Green Smoothie Detox is a perfect way to start the detox routine, especially if you are a newbie to the world of cleansing. For most people, the third day is the hardest, and maintaining your self-control becomes difficult. On the other hand, there are those that want to keep on with it once they reach the third day, because they are starting to feel so good.

However, it is best to stop after 3 days, and allow your body to read-just to its new state of well-being. By the end of the third day you will usually be feeling clean, rejuvenated and full of new energy. Just know this: It's only 3 days out of your life, after all, and you might just find that you like it.

Hint: If you have a friend that is familiar with Green Smoothies, and wants to clean up the old body or just lose a couple of pounds, then the buddy system is a great way to detox. You gain a shoulder to lean on and the tow of you can support one another through the process.

Here are a few things you can do to get ready for your 3 Day Green Smoothie Detox.

Consult with your physician before beginning any detox program. This is most important if you have any chronic health issues that could be affected in any way.

You have to get the right mindset going. Be determined and committed. Try checking out some testimonials online from others who have successfully done a 3 day detox, and read about all the wonderful things they have to say. It might be just the thing to get you in the right mood to succeed.

Schedule your 3 Day Green Smoothie Detox on a weekend or holiday, when you won't be expected at work. Detoxing causes frequent bodily elimination and sometimes nausea the first time you do it. It's best to stick close to home. (That's where all of your Green Smoothie foods are anyway.)

Rest up – Green Smoothies in general, and the detox smoothies in particular, give you lots of energy and you may have trouble falling asleep.

Drink lots and lots of water. It's an old cliché, I know, but it is oh so true. The best way to have your water is bottled or purified, with lemon. (After all, we're trying to get rid of the chemicals in our bodies, not add more with tap water.) If you are exceptionally brave, add a little all-natural apple cider vinegar to that lemon mix. It has to be unprocessed, unpasteurized and unfiltered. (Available in the health food aisle at your local grocers.) This is the best way to have your water every day, anyway, and it jump starts the flushing of your kidneys and digestive system, while it is super hydrating you. Besides, if you add a little sweetener, the lemon totally disguises the taste of the vinegar, and you'll never even know it is in there.

Cut out the caffeine by gradually decreasing it in the week prior to your planned detox. Sudden cessation of caffeine can cause headaches and a variety of other withdrawal symptoms. You may find after finishing your detox, that you don't even need that caffeine anymore.

Try to take the same week and cut down or eliminate sugar, fats, dairy products and unhealthy carbs from your diet. Stop already with the rice, the pasta, processed and canned foods, fast food, alcohol, sugar and anything that contains trans-fat.

Plan your eating schedule, activities and your recipes before you start. Make sure that you have filled your shopping list with everything you need for the 3 days. Include time for exercise and rest in that schedule. **HAVE IT ALL WRITTEN DOWN AND BE DETERMINED TO STICK TO IT.**

Get rid of any foods that you like and you know are not good for you, before you shop for your Green Smoothie detox foods. Don't give yourself a reason to give in to temptation.

Tip: If you really want to do a 3 Day Green Smoothie Detox and you are just not sure that you can handle it alone, go online and check out some of the Green Smoothie websites and join a 3 Day Challenge. They go on all the time and are very easy to find.

Learn from the past, set vivid, detailed goals for the future, and live in the only moment of time over which you have any control: now.

– Denis Waitley

Cautions & Possible Side Effects

While the 3 Day Green Smoothie Detox is safe and natural, it is something that your body won't be used to if you are new to this type of health program. The side effects are not serious and many people do not even experience any. However, it is always best to be forewarned, rather than possibly unpleasantly surprised.

Hint: You have to remember that when you detox for the first time, and if you are not a regular Green Smoothie fanatic, you will have cravings for the sugar, fat and carbs in the food you normally eat. This is a form of withdrawal, and so you can expect that there may be at least a few mild side effects. Don't let them stop you, because they will be gone in a day or so.

The usual side effects that people report when detoxing are:
- Lightheadedness
- Nausea
- Bloating
- Stomachache
- Diarrhea
- Headache
- Metallic taste in the mouth

- Mild skin breakouts
- Hunger, or rather the desire to chew on something solid

The hunger issue can be resolved by making sure you have your Green Smoothies for each meal, and a snack or two in between. The remaining side effects are extremely temporary, lasting only a day or two. They are caused by the toxins being eliminated from your body, and the increase in the fiber you are consuming in Green Smoothies. Your body will adjust very quickly and the symptoms will disappear.

IMPORTANT INFORMATION ABOUT GREENS: Greens in the brassica family such as, kale, cabbage and turnips contain gluco-sinates, spinach and beet greens contain oxalic acid; both of these substances are actually mild toxins naturally contained in the plants. They are the plant's natural self-defense against extinction in the wild. They are perfectly harmless and do provide health benefits to humans, as long as they are not consumed in overly large quantities. 2 bunches a day of any of them is fine, but the same greens should not be eaten every single day. Use at least 7 varieties of greens per week. Choosing from a variety of greens will make sure that you get all of the nutritional benefits that greens offer. Rotate those greens, and make sure you are rotating more than one plant family, instead of greens within the same family.

Important: You should consult with your medical professional before beginning any detox or diet. The 3 Day Green Smoothie Detox is not recommended for those in any of the following categories.

- Anemia
- Diabetes
- Kidney Disease
- Pregnant or Nursing
- Eating Disorders
- Laxative Use
- Athletes Competing in Sporting Events

Note: If you take prescription medications for any chronic medical condition, NEVER stop taking your medication in preparation for, or during a detox. Many medications must be maintained at certain levels in the body, and this only happens by taking them as prescribed. If you were to discontinue taking them it could have serious or even fatal consequences.

Optimism is the faith that leads to achievement. Nothing can be done without hope and confidence.

— Helen Keller

3 Day Green Smoothie Detox Shopping List

There are basically 7 things that you need to put together your Green Smoothie Detox.

1. A Blender
2. Chopping board
3. Sharp knife
4. Greens and other vegetables
5. Fruit
6. Water
7. Additives (nuts, seeds, superfoods, herbs, spices and extracts)

Greens contain loads of fiber, which is the nutrient that is responsible, on a daily basis for proper elimination of toxins from your digestive system. They are also one of the only food sources for Vitamin K. They contain many other vitamins and minerals and even antioxidants. Parsley has long been used as a natural detox food. Add parsley to any smoothie anytime for its natural detox properties. It also has a very mild flavor. Dandelion greens are powerful cleansers. Kale contains a phytonutrient that is believed to prevent many diseases and it contains Vitamin K. Romaine lettuce is wonderful for its fiber and its water content. Baby spinach is also a mild flavored and nutritious green.

Fruit is full of vitamins, antioxidants, phytonutrients, minerals, fiber and water. It needs to be ripe and fresh or frozen. Never use fruit juice for a detox because it has no fiber left in it. When detoxing, using berries is fine, you just have to use a lot since their fiber content is not as high. However, they do provide more water. A balance of different fruits and fruit types is the ticket to an effective detox Green Smoothie. Some of the most effective fruits for detoxification are: citrus fruits; lemons, limes, grapefruits and oranges, which have natural cleansing properties and lots of water. Pineapple is also a good choice because it contains the enzyme bromelain, which digests protein.

Hint: Citrus fruit is tart and rather sour. When you add greens the taste of the smoothie can be a little bitter. You can exchange ½ grapefruit for 1 orange and the smoothie will be sweeter. Try extra banana, raw honey or Stevia if it just won't get sweet enough to suit you.

Whenever possible try to use organic and farm fresh fruit, greens and vegetables, at least when you are detoxing. Grocery store produce may contain different levels of toxins from pesticides and fertilizers which can delay the effectiveness of your detox.

Nuts & Seeds–Additives such as seeds, nuts, avocado and coconut contain healthy fats that your body needs during detox to produce energy. These fats should not exceed 10 or 15% of your caloric intake when you detox. Superfoods like Chia Seeds, Goji Berries and Sprouts (which qualify as a green, by the way) are excellent sources of extra nutrients and fiber.

Herbs–(also considered greens) add nutrition, flavor and healing properties. Spices and extracts can enhance the flavor of your smoothie and help to personalize a recipe to suit your taste buds.

Water–is always necessary for hydration, and necessary to preparing a perfect Green Smoothie. During a detox it is even more important. You can also have coconut water and caffeine free teas such as ginger, Peppermint Tea and other herbal teas. Unless you live by a natural stream of fresh water, try to using filtered or mineral water to avoid different toxins that may exist in tap water.

The first step in putting together your 3 Day Green Smoothie Detox shopping list is to go to the recipe section and pick out enough recipes to last for the whole 3 days.

The second step is to make a list of all the ingredients that you will need to prepare those recipes.

The third step is to go through the foods, spices etc. that you already have, and check them off the list.

Whatever is left on your list is what you need to shop for.

You may be asking yourself "Where is the shopping list"? Don't worry, I didn't forget to include it here!

The reason its not here is due to the fact that some items may already be hiding in your kitchen while others may be things you would never be caught eating. Furthermore, some ingredients are harder to find or more expensive than others. That's why I equipped you with many different recipes that will suit every taste bud and allow you the freedom of choice.

Hint: This is also the time to remove any foods from your home that might tempt you while you are on the 3 Day Green Smoothie Detox program. If temptation sets in, it is just too easy to give in, if you have things that are not healthy, or not included in your recipes, on hand.

Are you ready to start your green smoothie detox?

Even if you fall on your face, you're still moving forward.

– Victor Kiam

Step By Step
3 Day Green
Smoothie Detox

Here are a few Tips to get the most from your 3 Day Green Smoothie Detox

1. Water, Water, Water. Drink as much as you can, not just in your smoothies, but in addition to them. Your body has a larger percentage of water than anything else. Staying hydrated is especially important when detoxifying, because you have a continuous flush going on.

2. Make sure to get plenty of sleep. 7 or 8 hours a night is necessary for your body to rest and rejuvenate. Take naps during your detox if you need to.

3. Stick to the plan. The 3 Day Green Smoothie Detox plan works best if you do everything at the same times each day. It encourages the body to operate regularly. Rise and go to bed at the same time each day and have your smoothie meals and snacks at the same time.

4. Get some Exercise. During a detox, you may want to tone down your workout routine a little, but you do need to get at least some mild exercise during your detox. The more exercise you can comfortably do, the more weight you may lose.

5. Pick out a book you've been meaning to read, or drag out your crafting supplies. Get out the old ink pen and write some real letters, surf the net or watch some movies that you have wanted to see. Plan to do things that you enjoy, and that you normally don't have the time or patience for. This is a great way to spend your time during your 3 day detox.

6. Weigh-In – Weigh yourself the first thing on Day1 after rising. Then begin your detox. Keep a record of your weight, weigh every night right before bed. I think you'll be surprised at the end of Day 3.

7. For the purposes of our 3 Day Green Smoothie Detox, we will be going on the presumption that we are on holiday or a long weekend, so that we do not have to prepare our Green Smoothies in advance and store them. We want to get the full nutritional value from them.

Hint: Your size and your appetite will determine how much smoothie you will need in a day. For me it is 80 to 120 ounces of Green Smoothie per day during detox. Just remember that you can have another anytime you get hungry; this is not a starvation diet. If a recipe makes too much, have half now and the other half a little later. Any time you feel hungry you can have another Green Smoothie. Nothing is set in stone.

Day 1

7:00 AM – Get up and weigh-in. Prepare a morning Green Smoothie. While you are doing this have a glass of lemon water and/or a cup of Tea. Have your smoothie.

9:30 AM – Do some deep breathing exercises. Have a large glass of lemon water. You can have a Green Smoothie snack now if you need one.

12:00 PM – Time to make your lunch Green Smoothie and enjoy it. Have more lemon water and some Green or Peppermint Tea.

2:30 PM – Have a 15 to 30 minute walk, and top it off with a large glass of lemon water. Have another Green Smoothie snack if you like.

5:00 PM – Have your large Green Smoothie dinner now. You can have the regular cold Green Smoothie or whip up a batch of Green Smoothie Soup.

7:30 PM – Have a green smoothie snack, if you need one, or a soothing cup of herbal tea. You don't want to wake up in the night starving.

10:00 PM – An hour before bed is a great time to dry brush your skin and shower. Get all the toxins off your skin before you sleep.

11:00 PM – Bedtime. Don't forget to weigh-in before you lie down, and make a note of it. Keep a carafe or bottle of fresh water nearby so that you can hydrate if you wake in the night. Set the alarm for 7:00 AM.

Day 2

In Day 2 we will keep to the same schedule as Day 1. However, we want to vary our exercise. This is how to do it.

7:00 AM – Get up and weigh-in. Prepare a morning Green Smoothie. While you are doing this have a glass of lemon water and/or a cup of Herbal Tea. Have your smoothie.

9:30 AM – Same as Day 1. I like to do the deep breathing at this time each morning, but on Day 2, I add a little exercise. I do 10 leg lifts on each leg and 20 curls on each arm with a 6 pound dumbbell.

12:00 PM – Time to make your lunch Green Smoothie and enjoy it. Have more lemon water and some Green or Peppermint Tea.

2:30 PM – Same as Day 1. Instead of a walk I ride my exercise bike for 20 to 30 minutes. You can also ride a bicycle out of doors if you prefer.

5:00 PM – Have your large Green Smoothie dinner now. You can have the regular cold Green Smoothie or whip up a batch of Green Smoothie Soup.

7:30 PM – Same as Day 1. I just add a walk before having a Green Smoothie snack. I take a 15 to 20 minute walk around the neighborhood. If you have a treadmill, you can use that instead.

10:00 PM – I like to add deep breathing on Day 2, before I dry brush and shower.

11:00 PM – Same as Day 1. Don't forget to weigh-in and write it down.

Hint: As you can see, what I am doing is increasing the exercise each day a little, because I love to find out at the end of 3 days that I have actually lost weight.

Day 3

By Day 3 it may be a getting a little tough to stick it out one more day, but, hey this is the last one, and you will have successfully completed your first Green Smoothie Detox. So, hang in there, and we'll get through it.

Day 3 is just like Day 1 and 2, except we add a little more physical activity. The addition of exercise not only promotes your weight loss goals, but it actually helps to remove the toxins in your body. This is a very important part of your detox routine.

7:00 AM – On this final morning, I want to be in a great mood and feel really good. So when I first get up I make sure I do deep breathing and about 5 minutes of stretching, then have my water/herbal Tea, before I have my Green Smoothie.

9:30 AM – This is the same as Day 1 and Day 2 except that I increase my exercise to include 15 leg lifts on each leg.

12:00 PM – After lunch on Day 3, I take a 10 to 15 minute walk.

2:30 PM – Same as Day 1. Instead of a walk I ride my exercise bike for 20 to 30 minutes. You can also ride a bicycle out of doors if you prefer.

5:00 PM – Have your large Green Smoothie dinner now. You can have the regular cold Green Smoothie or whip up a batch of Green Smoothie Soup.

7:30 PM – Same as Day 1 and Day 2. I try to increase my walk to 30 minutes.

10:00 PM – I add 10 minutes of stretching, after my deep breathing, and before my dry brush and shower.

11:00 PM – Weigh-In, don't forget to keep water handy and Have A Great Night.

Hint: There is no such thing as too much deep breathing. Do it several times a day. Oxygen in = Carbon Dioxide Out. Carbon dioxide is a toxin to the human body, just like any other.

Exercise – Your exercise does not have to be the same as mine. I like to walk and ride my bike, but I also throw around a kettle ball, jump rope and do a little Tae Bo. If you go to aerobics class or practice yoga, do that. If you lift weights or run and you feel like it, do it. The idea is to get moving. It enhances your detox and your health in general. It helps your body to complete all of its necessary processes in a more efficient manner.

Dry Brushing – This is absolutely wonderful for your skin. Your skin also expels toxins, and dry brushing helps to remove them from the pores. Use a soft and gentle natural bristle brush. Never scrub at your skin, as this will just damage it, and that kind of defeats the purpose. You can find an appropriate brush at health food stores or online.

There are many commercially available cleansing products, juice fasts, water fasts, lemonade diets and a million others. What do they all have in common? They do not provide the nutrition that your body needs to feel and look its best. Most of them will make you feel terrible and/or spend all of your time in the bathroom.

Not only is this not practical, it is simply not healthy to deny your body the nutrients and energy it needs. Will these other detox programs kill you? Probably not, but you might wish you were dead before you are through with them. Would I recommend any of them? Absolutely not.

Everything You Need To Know About Blenders

The only appliance you need for smoothies is a blender. Most people already own a blender and you can use the one you have. Of course, there are many nifty blenders out there to choose from, and some are even designed for making smoothies. However, fancy blenders come with fancy prices, so I don't recommend running right out to purchase one of these, unless you are positive that you will continue to make smoothies.

For making smoothies, power is the main issue. Powerful blenders make smoother and creamier textured smoothies. That is the ideal consistency that we are aiming for. The power of the blender will determine the amount of liquid ingredients that must be added.

High powered blenders use more liquid because they are much more thorough at liquefying the ingredients. Lower powered (translates to cheaper) blenders require far less or no liquid at all. However, your smoothie may not have the exact consistency that you desire. There are ways to solve this problem, other than buying an expensive new blender. Since you control the ingredients, then you have control over the results.

These are features you should look for if you purchase a new blender for smoothies:

Power – As much power as you can get. This makes smoothies far easier to make. A cheap blender, that has little power, will make it difficult to get the proper smoothie consistency. You will need to chop, grate or mash the ingredients before adding them.

Tamping Tool – This is a marvelous invention that lets you push the ingredients down closer to the blade without tangling in it. This is an option to look for, but it will probably be more common on blenders that cost more.

Quality – You do not want plastic gears turning the blade. It is too easy for them to strip out. Then you would have to buy another, and you can't save money like that. The blender should be well built and sturdy, with a decent warranty.

Blenders can cost from about $25, to well over $1000. Here is a comparison.

Inexpensive Blenders – You can get it cheap and it will work. This option does have its drawbacks. Cheap blenders have the plastic gear that you don't want. They usually wear out or strip out very quickly. You have to run a cheap blender longer to achieve the result you want, so it is safe to assume that it won't last long before the motor burns up. Continually replacing the blender is not going to save any money in the long run, not to mention that it takes more time and prep work.

Mid-Range Blender – This would be the $200 to $500 blender, which is a good choice. It will last longer than the cheap blender, but costs less than the specialty blenders. It is also more powerful and well-built. Be wary of the quality. Blenders in this price range will sometimes be very good, but some are just a brand name that won't deliver the goods. Do your research and check online user reviews before you make a choice.

Expensive Blenders – This is the $500 to well over $1000 price range. If you are not a dedicated smoothie maker, you may not want to go here. Make sure you really want to invest in a blender if you are thinking about purchasing one of these. Bells and whistles – check. Just make sure you are actually going to use it often.

My advice is to just use whatever blender you already have, for now. If you prepare your ingredients properly and follow the 8 steps to a perfect smoothie, then you can take your time deciding whether you really need another blender or not.

Always do your best. What you plant now, you will harvest later.

– Og Mandino

Detox Recipes

Select recipes that have ingredients that you like. Just make sure that you get a wide variety of ingredients and don't use the same recipe more than once during the 3 days.

Don't forget that you can add Chia Seeds, Flax Seeds, Wheat Germ, Pumpkin Seeds, Nuts, Herbs, Spices and Extracts to customize any 3 Day Green Smoothie Detox Recipe.

Hint: The more frozen fruits that you use, the colder and thicker your smoothie will be. You can also replace water with crushed ice.

Green Smoothie Making Tip: All Green Smoothies are prepared the same way. Place all of the ingredients except the Greens in the blender and pulse a few times. Then add the Greens and process on high until you have a smooth and creamy texture.

#1 Simple Green Smoothie

This is the easiest Green Smoothie ever, and it lends itself well to customizing the flavors.

> 2 Bananas, frozen
> 1 Peach, peeled and pitted
> 5 Strawberries, frozen
> 3 handfuls Baby Spinach or other Greens
> 1 cup Water

Makes 1 Serving

#2 Wake-Up Green Smoothie

This is an energizing and delicious Green Smoothie, just perfect first thing in the morning.

> 2 Bananas, frozen
> 5 Plums, peeled and pitted
> 3 cups Water
> 1 handful Baby Spinach
> 2 handfuls Kale

Makes 4 servings of 14 to 16 ounces

#3 Purple Power Breakfast Green Smoothie

Absolutely delicious and great for Day 3 breakfast, gives you lots of energy.

> 1 Apple, peeled and cored
> 4 cups Pineapple, fresh, peeled and cored
> 1 cup Blueberries, frozen
> 3 cups Water
> 1 pound Baby Spinach or any Green
> 3 tbsp. Flax Seeds

Makes 70 Ounces

#4 Mango-Pear Green Smoothie

Sweet and tasty, this one is perfect for lunch or snacks.

> 1 large Mango, peeled and pitted
> 2 Pears, peeled and cored
> 3 cups Water
> 1 handful Purple Kale
> 2-3 handfuls Chard

Makes 50 Ounces

#5 Strawberry Aloe Vera Green Smoothie

This is a great choice for lunch; light, fresh and fabulous.

> 4 cups Strawberries, frozen
> 2 Pears, peeled and cored

3 ounces Aloe Vera Juice

3 cups water

½ tsp. Cardamom

2 tsp. Pure Vanilla Extract

1 large head Romaine Lettuce (1 pound or more)

Makes 80 Ounces

#6 Orange Beets Green Smoothie

Delightful and different; this one packs an energizing wallop.

1 Large Ripe Mango, peeled and pitted

3 Oranges, peeled and seeded

1/2 cup Aloe Vera Juice

3 cups Water

2 handfuls Beet Greens with purple stems

1 tbsp. Flax Seeds

Makes 4 Servings

#7 My Darling Clementine Green Smoothie

The unusual combination of Clementines and Plums is unbeatable.

4 Clementines, peeled and seeded

2 Plums, peeled and pitted

1 cup Water or Crushed Ice

2 tbsp. each Flax Seeds and Chia Seeds

4 cups Greens (your choice)

Makes 2 Servings

#8 Pineapple & Radish Greens Smoothie

Did you know that the greens of the radish were a great option and chock full of nutrition?

2 Bananas, frozen and peeled

1 ripe Mango, peeled and pitted

1/2 ripe Pineapple, peeled and cored

3 cups Water or Crushed Ice

3 handfuls Radish Greens

1/2 cup Goji Berries

3 tbsp. Flax Seeds

2 tbsp. Wheat Germ

Makes 64 Ounces

#9 Orange Goji Green Smoothie

1 Orange, peeled and seeded

2 Dates, pitted and chopped

3 tbsp. Goji Berries

1 cup Water or Crushed Ice

3 cups Mixed Dark Greens (or your choice)

1 tbsp. Wheat Germ

Makes 20 Ounces

#10 Orange Cream Green Smoothie Snack

This one is a fabulous choice for your snack times; you'll think you've had ice cream.

1 Orange, peeled and seeded

¼ Avocado, peeled and pitted

1 cup Nut Milk or Coconut Water

1 handful each Romaine Lettuce and Baby Spinach

½ tsp. Pure Vanilla Extract

Sweetener to taste if needed

Makes 1 Serving

#11 Plum Bananas Green Smoothie

You will go "plum bananas" over this taste bud titillating treat.

4 Plums, peeled and pitted

2 Bananas, frozen and peeled

2 Oranges, peeled and seeded

4 Dates, chopped

3 cups Water

4 handfuls Bok Choy

3 tbsp. Flax Seeds

3 tbsp. Goji Berries

Makes 64 Ounces

#12 Raspy Orange Green Smoothie

A little different and a whole lot tasty.

2 Oranges, peeled and seeded

2 cups Raspberries, fresh or frozen

8 Dates, pitted and chopped for sweetness or to taste

1 tbsp. Chia Seeds

2 cups Water

5 handfuls Lambsquarters or your choice of greens

Makes 36 Ounces

#13 Green on Green Smoothie

This one is a real fiber and protein miracle that still manages to be tasty.

6 Dates, pitted and chopped

1 Banana, frozen and peeled

½ Avocado, peeled and pitted

3 tbsp. Flax Seeds

3 tbsp. Wheat Germ

2 cups water

2 cups Bok Choy

Makes 24 Ounces

#14 Sweet and Tasty Mustard Green Smoothie

1 Banana, frozen and peeled

1 Orange, peeled and seeded

1 large Fuji Apple, peeled and cored

6 Figs, chopped

3 cups water

4 handfuls Mustard Greens

3 tbsp. Wheat Germ

3 tbsp. Flax Seeds

Makes 50 Ounces

#15 Bananalicious Green Smoothie
If you love bananas, this is the one for you.

    4 Bananas, frozen and peeled

    1 cup Raspberries, frozen

    6 Dates, pitted and chopped

    4 cups Water

    2 large bunches Dark Green Lettuce

    3 tbsp. Chia Seeds

    2 tbsp. Wheat Germ

Makes 60 Ounces

#16 Raspberry Dandelions Green Smoothie
Tart raspberries and dandelion green nutrition is a winning combo.

    1 Banana, frozen and peeled

    2 cups Raspberries, frozen

    5 Figs, chopped

    3 cups water

    1full bunch Dandelion Greens

Makes 2 to 3 Servings

#17 Energizer Bunny Green Smoothie
You might find it really hard to be still after this one. Try it before exercise and you'll be amazed how fast the time goes by.

    2 Bananas, frozen and peeled

    6 Dates, pitted and chopped

    2 cups Water

    2 large bunches Dark Green Lettuce

    2 heaping tbsp. Wheat Germ

    3 tbsp. Flax Seeds

Makes 40 Ounces

#18 Aloe Parsley Green Smoothie

Mildly flavored, yet sweet and fruity; this one is a winner.

        2 Bananas, frozen and peeled
        1 Orange, peeled and seeded
        1 each Apple and Pear, peeled and cored
        2 cups Water
        ¼ cup Aloe Vera Juice
        1 handful each Baby Spinach, Bok Choy and Curly Parsley
        2 tbsp. each Flax and Chia Seeds

Makes 2 Servings

#19 Melon Lovers Dream Green Smoothie

This is a super cleansing smoothie with all the goodness of sweet melons.

        2 Bananas, frozen and peeled
        2 cups Cantaloupe, peeled, seeded and cubed
        1 cup Watermelon, seeded
        1 cup Honeydew Melon, seeded and cubed
        3 cups Water
        5 handfuls greens (your choice)
        ¼ cup Sesame Seeds 3 tbsp. Wheat Germ

Makes 55+ Ounces

#20 Berry Kale Creamy Green Smoothie

Assorted berries, bananas and Kale are a delicious combination sure to please.

        2 Bananas, frozen and peeled
        2 cups Strawberries, 1 cup Blueberries, frozen
        4 to 6 Dates, pitted and chopped
        2 cups Water
        1 large bunch Kale
        2 tbsp. Flax Seeds

Makes 50 Ounces

#21 Super Iron Power Green Smoothie

If you need to get some extra iron in your detox, this is just the way to do it.

>2 cups Honeydew, peeled, seeded and cubed
>1 Banana, frozen and peeled
>1 Mango, peeled, pitted and cubed
>1 cup Water
>11 ounces Coconut Water
>5 handfuls Kale
>¼ cup each Chia, Flax and Sesame Seeds

Makes about 50 Ounces

Bonus Recipes

These recipes are great as Dinner replacements!

These recipes are made with hot water, and can be eaten from a bowl like soup. They concentrate on vegetables accented with spices, so they seem more like dinner. Have them along with a fruit smoothie for a beverage and you have a satisfying, filling dinner that won't leave you feeling that you have missed a thing.

Hint: Any spice that you normally use for vegetable dishes will be perfect additions to these soup smoothies. Try onion, garlic, sea salt, black pepper, cayenne, basil, thyme, or whatever you prefer.

#1 Savory Green Dinner Soup Smoothie

This one is very filling and will remind you of meatless vegetable soup.

> 2 Tomatoes
> 3 Carrots, chopped
> 4 stalks Celery, chopped
> 1 small Onion, peeled and chopped
> 2 handfuls each Kale and Baby Spinach
> 1 handful Parsley
> 2 cups Hot Water

Fresh Garlic, sea salt, black pepper, cayenne or other to taste

If not warm enough to suit, heat for a few seconds in the microwave.

Makes 2 Large Bowls

#2 Lemony Basil Green Soup Smoothie

Lemon and basil are a classic culinary combination, and make a delicious dinner soup smoothie.

> 2 Carrots, chopped
> 2 Stalks Celery, chopped
> 1 head Broccoli, chopped
> ½ ripe Avocado, peeled and pitted
> 5 handfuls Greens 1 handful Sprouts
> 1 fresh Lemon, juiced
> Hot Water to desired consistency
> 1 Tsp. Basil 1 Garlic Clove, chopped
> Sea salt, Black Pepper, Oregano to taste

Makes 2 Large Bowls

#3 Green Smoothie Curry Soup

If you love curried dishes then this is the one for you.

> 4 Carrots, chopped
> 4 stalks Celery, chopped
> ½ Cucumber, peeled and chopped
> 2 handfuls Greens
> 1 handful Parsley
> ¼ cup Cashews, chopped
> Hot Water as needed
> Ginger, Garlic, Sea Salt and Curry Powder to taste

Makes 2 Large Bowls

More Smoothie Recipes

These 3 recipes are great additions to the Dinner replacement recipes **Hint:** You can add greens to these smoothies as well, and they will be more filling and nutritious.

#1 Banana Berry Dream

Sweet, sweet, sweet; a drink and dessert in one.

  1 Banana, frozen
  1 Peach, peeled and pitted
  2 cups Berries, frozen, mixed or single (strawberries, blueberries, raspberries, etc.)
  ½ Tsp. Pure Vanilla or Almond Extract

Makes 2 Servings

#2 Tropical Papamango Delight Smoothie

If you like the taste and scent of a tropical island, this one is for you.

  1 Banana, frozen
  1 Mango, peeled and pitted
  1 Papaya, peeled and seeded
  1 Orange, peeled and seeded

1 cup Fresh Pineapple, peeled and cored
1 cup Coconut Water
1 cup Crushed Ice

Makes 2 Large Servings

#3 Happy Apple Smoothie

This fruit smoothie will remind you of an apple pie; maybe it is dessert, or is it a drink?

2 Bananas, frozen
2 Apples, peeled, cored and chopped
2 Dates or 2 Figs, chopped
¼ cup Almonds, chopped
1 tsp. Pure Vanilla Extract
Cinnamon and Nutmeg to taste
Crushed Ice if needed to chill or thicken

Makes 2 Large Servings

Tip to improve Green Smoothie Detox and Nutrition: Throw in some sprouts when you make your Green Smoothies. Not only are they another Green, they also contain more nutrients and enzymes than fully grown plants. It is easy to sprout edible seeds yourself in a glass jar with a screened lid. Here are some favorites:

- Wheat Berries
- Alfalfa
- Radish
- Broccoli
- Flax seeds

Hint: The Aloe Vera juice used in Green Smoothie recipes is from a particular variety of Aloe Vera plant that is edible. Make sure you are using the correct plant juice.

Green Smoothie FAQs

#1 Why should I do a 3 Day Green Smoothie Detox?

Everything that you eat, that your skin comes in contact with and even the air that you breathe, is full of chemicals and other substances that are poisonous to the human body. Without assistance, the body cannot rid itself of these toxins. Toxins eventually cause serious or even fatal diseases. They make you feel generally bad, cause you stress, and can even harm your mood and mental agility. Without proper detoxification in a healthy way, you will never look or feel your best, and weight loss programs will never be truly effective, or help you obtain lasting results. It is all about the proper nutrition that you get from Green Smoothies. There are many detox programs, but only one that is truly healthy and works perfectly every time.

#2 Will I have side effects from a Green Smoothie Detox?

While you can experience mild disturbances in digestion and sleeping habits, among others when you first begin the Green Smoothie detox, they will not last more than a day or two, and then you will feel better than ever. Many people never have the first symptom of a side effect. The benefits far outweigh any initial mild discomfort. This is just the body adjusting to proper nutrition.

#3 Will the Green Smoothie detox really help me lose weight?

Almost everyone who follows the 3 Day Green Smoothie Detox loses some weight. It can range from only a pound or two, and as much as 9 pounds has been reported by people doing this detox. If you continue with Green Smoothies as part of a healthy diet on a daily basis, the weight will begin to drop off. Green Smoothies are all nutrition and no crap that the body does not need.

#4 How often, and for how long, should I Detox?

This can vary according to the individual. Detox can be done for 3 to 7 days. I recommend the 3 Day Detox. It will get the job done, especially if Green Smoothies are a part of your regular diet, because you will literally be detoxing all the time. I do the 3 day program 4 times per year, once each season. You can also add a one day detox after a large holiday meal or other event, when you feel that you have really overdone it with the food.

#5 How can that green goop, that you call a Green Smoothie, taste good?

Green Smoothies taste good because of the way you combine the ingredients, and the fact that you mix fruit with your Greens. As a matter of fact, you use a lot of sweet and tasty fruits, and they totally overpower the taste of the Greens.

In Conclusion

Now that you have completed your first 3 Day Green Smoothie Detox, it is time to add Green Smoothies to your everyday routine, so that you can continue to feel this rejuvenated and energized. Just replace one or two meals a day and a snack with a healthy Green Smoothie and you will pretty much stay detoxified.

When I first discovered Green Smoothies, I could feel the very first one while I was still in the process of consuming it. I thought to myself: there must really be something to this Green Smoothie thing. I believe in Green Smoothie nutrition with all of my heart, and I hope that you are a believer now, too.

It still amazes me, when I think about how simple foods that were already in my diet could cause such drastic changes in my life, and all I had to do was learn to prepare and combine them in a different way. It also stuns me that I can look at what I used to consider "my favorite foods," and feel no desire whatsoever to eat them.

Other than the positive changes Green Smoothies have made in the way that I look and feel, I absolutely adore being able to leave the stove and the dirty dishes behind most of the time. Green Smoothies are the perfect solution for a busy lifestyle on the go. It takes less than 15 minutes to prepare a Green Smoothie meal or snack, instead of standing over a hot stove for an hour, and then still having to clean up the mess. This allows me so much more time to do the things that I really love to do.

And let's consider the grocery bill. Most of the fresh foods that I buy, I would have bought anyway, but now I have no need to buy massive amounts of expensive meat, dairy and processed foods. While the additives that I use in my Green Smoothies, such as Goji Berries and Chia Seeds are not cheap, they last a long time because you only use small amounts. The bottom line is that in addition to the health benefits, a Green Smoothie way of life actually does save me money.

I sincerely hope that you have taken away from this experience, and that you will continue to pursue the Green Smoothie way of life for your own benefit.

Get Your Free Bonus Below!

To get instant access to your free e-course *"10 Days To Everlasting Health"* either click the link below if you are reading the digital version:

http://greensmoothies.me/freecourse

Or manually copy the URL directly to your internet browser!

Additional Green Smoothie Resources

The New Green Smoothie Diet Solution
Now Available Both On Amazon Kindle & Paperback
A complete whole-food diet blueprint about green smoothies, their benefits, how to prepare them, store them and a collection of flavor packed recipes!

Pure Green: 100+ Delicious Green Smoothie Recipes
Now Available Both On Amazon Kindle & Paperback
A hand picked collection of over 100 easy to prepare, budget friendly recipes!

About The Author

Elizabeth Swann (Miller) has over 10 years of experience as a practicing Naturopath (ND) specializing in healing through nutrition. She has degrees both in Psychology and Naturopathy.

As a person struggling with overweight throughout her childhood, teens and early 20's, Elizabeth decided to take charge, take stock and start making changes in her life for the better.

Her experiences with thousands of clients and her own personal experiences have led her to become an author. Her goal is to educate as many people as possible about the healing powers of food and how to easily incorporate these changes into daily life.

Elizabeth has two daughters and currently lives and practices in Mount Carmel in sunny Israel.

Want to talk with Elizabeth? Email her at: Elizabethswannbooks@gmail.com

Or visit her website at: http://greensmoothies.me

Made in the USA
Lexington, KY
23 October 2013